Star-crossed Lavenders

A Gallery of Poetry

Vaishnavi Chari

ISBN 978-93-5559-131-9
© Vaishnavi Chari 2021
Published in India 2021 by Pencil

Contributors:
Editor: Ramanuja Chari
Editor: Ramanuja Chari
Co-Author: Sudha Chari
Co-Author: Sudha Chari

A brand of
One Point Six Technologies Pvt. Ltd.
123, Building J2, Shram Seva Premises,
Wadala Truck Terminal, Wadala (E)
Mumbai 400037, Maharashtra, INDIA
E connect@thepencilapp.com
W www.thepencilapp.com

Author biography

Vaishnavi belongs to the majestic state of Maharashtra having a rich cultural-literary heritage. She's a poetess who loves to carve emotions into words. She has been inking her heart out since the second grade and believes to continue till aeons to come. Profession forced her into Microbiology while passion kept her connected to journals. She loves to inculcate imagery into reality blending them into beautiful poetry. Her mainstream is Hindi-English and she has a thing for Urdu nazms and ghazals. A staunch follower of Sri Krishna, she is inspired by reading the likes of Gulzar, Harivansh Rai, Shakespeare, Wordsworth, Shelley and Maupassant. Also a keen skygazer, a solivagant globetrotter and a myth-fiction enthusiast, she can be traced back to her gardens - penning verses..

CONTENTS

Epigraph

"..And all my poems start to sink-

Verse by verse, word by word;

giving my confessions

a narrow escape from reality-

Into the ocean of your eyes.

Behold me there forever -

I'd be glad to be bewitched

In their enchantment.."

..Love, even if as an allegory is defined as a bond, cannot thrive and flourish in bondage. It's when that person grants you wings of flight, you can really fall in love. Chains of domination make the ballad - a nightmare. Love is a hypnosis, a trance wherein you just cannot shoo away the pleasant thoughts of your beloved..

Foreword

Jai Sree Krśna..!

"The world seeks your refuge, I seek your refuge

Karmanye vadhikaraste Ma Phaleshu Kadachana

Ma Karmaphalaheturbhurma Te Sangostvakarmani

2-47

TRANSLITERATION

Your right is to perform your work, but never to the results. Never be motivated by the results of your actions, nor should you be attached to not performing your prescribed duties.

"The woods were lovely dark and deep

But I have promises to keep

And miles to go before I sleep

And miles to go before I sleep."

Robert Frost

Preface

Interpretations or judgements are never honest. We never purely express the things we feel directly from our heart. We never appreciate the things we like yet always criticise the things we object to. This may be called as the human psyche. We, as humans may be unwilling to boost others future or progress by openly favouring them while we are always ready to bring down others confidence by consistently nagging them. This is where we try to judge people. We all have our own assessment of the people we meet daily. We all have their respective subconscious images sketched into our brains. And when the time comes to judge their actions, this analysis comes to the rescue. Our views about others is always backed by the latter's impression they have cast upon us knowingly or unknowingly.

Again, not all the people who praise, do it to genuinely express their appreciation. Some even praise to merely grab the eyeballs-to just qualify as the 'being in good books' type of person. And yes, not all the people who don't praise, are the people with lack of sensitivity or are leg pullers. Some people just aren't able to express their opinions due to the fear of judgement. And that, most importantly shouldn't be misinterpreted - even if it be left uninterpreted.

This book for me is a dream meet it's destiny. Kt consists all the poems I'd written in my initial years, from 2004 to 2008, hoping to see them in print someday. Like the union of two star crossed lovers in the wrecked sea of fulfilment. Dreams are realms of incomplete thoughts if not fulfilled in the chronology of time. This book for me is like a sweet lover whose thought I've nourished since times I cannot recall now. Being spectators of this union, O people! You are evidences and witnesses of this holy union.

Before starting this I was indebted to the master artists and wordsmiths of classical and contemporary times who've been a source of inspiration for many. This is a little effort to pay back to them the precious inheritance they've shared..

May the divinity inspire me to keep you all entertained throughout and bestow blessings onto this universe..!

Acknowledgements

The completion of this dream project of mine would not have seen execution without the support of my parents and my loved ones..

Their unfaltering belief, timely correction and age old inspiration coupled with continuous efforts and patience came together as a team in fulfilling this book.

A huge thanks to the publication team without whose coordinated and consecrated efforts, this dream would not have seen the dawn of completion. And above all thanks to The Almighty God for his unconditional love and omnipresent motivation..

Introduction

Ah! As John Keats had quoted long back- "A thing of beauty is a joy forever" - beautiful things always catch the fancy of artists, which they string in their art and present to the world. This obsession with beauty, however, when incorporated in love, becomes lustful. The beauty of love lies in unconditionality..

I'm blissful on this occasion to have been gratified by serving you O readers! I'm humbled by your recitals and blessed by your servitude.. Now I owe none !!

With Love and Reverence... To you, Dear Amma and Dearest Nanna

Ahh! Stars!

Ahh! How dear do those stars feel to me

Those icicles twinkling in a lover's eyes

Pronuncing love for the very first time

Devoid of conditions, rejection or avarice..

Or when he points to infinite constellations

Gazing into the mysteries of the universe,

Me finding my Muse in those sparkling clusters

And falling for his rusticity verse by verse..

Or the innumerous shooting stars that crash

In sheer lust for a mere union with the Earth,

Who innocent, unaware ignites them mercilessly

The meteors surrend to Her will in utter mirth..

Ah! Stars! Thou teach us beauty in strife;

That 'incessant blazing' brings out inner spark,

Or the constant Polaris which since aeons

Inspires us to create a niche and make a 'mark'..

Endowed with beauty and reservoirs of fire

'Astronomical angels' you seem to twin with me,

Oh the Creator of celestial yūgen art!

In genuine awe and reverence I bow to thee..

To the sore eyes of a disheartened maiden,

Who forgot to count the stars she wished upon,

Thou art a mere tool of an artists' fantasy

A disillusioned piece or the Destiny's pawn..

Reminescence

The disturbing disappointments struck a bond with failures

Endurance and patience taking a hurried reverse turn

Pushing me into sheer dense forests of unknown dakness

Tears evaporating into nothingnes, eyes beginning to burn

Who was the accused, who pleaded guilty, who innocent?

Messed colors mingled which bring the canvas of love to life

Or the intricate string of faith which relations tends to bind

The monochrome of loneliness was all I had managed to earn

Traversing across hushing silences, my mind again reminds

Reminiscence indeed !

Wounds the deepest and pricks in the most agonizing manner..

A poetic truce

A poem is not a sonnet

decorated in certain

incomplete verses

Or a means of escape

into an alternate reality

A poem is an outpouring

of emotions long latched

In chains of tranquillity

Fearing the ultimate doom

of a nurtured relation

A poem is not a story

Adorned in calligraphy

And recited in tones

Or deliberately forced

to fit in multiple rhymes

A poem is that emotion

Which a caged bird sings

In its utter loneliness

A pain that we can feel

In its fleeting melancholy

A poem is not a proposal

Strung in beautiful words

Said on behalf of a lover

to soothe his Muse

into the arms of deceit

A poem is the expression of love

Which unites two pining lovers

Long separated by distance

Yet finding solace in one another

Through the starry night

A poem is not a ballad

Or a tale of a knight

Or accounts of bravery told

across several generations

as a famous folklore

A poem is their achievement

which tends to inspire us

rekindling the fire of flight

in wings over weighed by failure

re-defining stamdards of success..

Approval

Confronting you I now kowtow

Trekking around my ways halt on you

Does this surmise you too?

None matter to me more than you

You are my prayer, you my wish

My universe is meaningless

You my everything, the world a foe..

Say for once for your words are script

I'd abide by all your ravishing ways

Walking on your footprints forgetting trays

If you'd say, I'd make vales drift

Translate to you the message of winds

Steal the sun of its golden cosmic Ray's

And stack them together as your gift..

Your incomplete eyes seem to hide a nightmare

Do they fear that I would be lured of you?

My heart recommends to move away

As if my breath forgets to breath it seems..

Nature's realms

Flawless floe for flattering flares

Verses vaunted via viciousness

Appearing artisans archaicly ascend

Intervening intruders in intersection

Icicles ignited in immense iridescence

Shallow showers sharing shrewd silence

Hindering heaven, hitherto hesitant

Nattering nightingales nurturing nuisance

Zillion zingy zinnia zapping zootopia's

Amber ambience. Azalea astirring alfresco

Around azure and amethyst aretes

Verdant valerian valley viz. vernal virtuoso

Intruding intrinsic illusionary ivy islets

Nestled neatly nullifying nuisance..

Enclosed within a graveyard - Autumn

Aeons seem to have passed since

The nightingale's last visit

Yet across these ways I mince

The roads swept by tides of time..

Footprints long casted still remain

As if under a wizard's influence

This valley- shall spring ever regain?

Or will these get lost in pages of history..?

The paths diverge into small tunnels

Weaving a complicated labyrinth

Walking past I watched the kernel

Of this place- a magical element..

Decayed leaves rustling in the breeze

Initiating a cyclone like situation

The willows moving in altruistic ease

Sheltered in the blanket of the night..

The day woke without dawn chorus

The woods grasped in eerie silence

Shock stricken I start progression

In the island of frightful graves..

Leaves jingle in a pathetic dirge

The lifeless trees restlessly move

Desires ceased to exhibit urge

Like randomly scattered clouds..

Displaying their menace over the valley

Their bow being the thunderbolt

The leaves formed a fading ally

Over the gateway of teriffic hell..

The howling wind growling fiercely

Sea waves imitating warning sirens

Tge unforeseen storm adversely

Brings the hope of a new season..

Spring being your own kindred

It seems too late to arrive

Hymns to it are offered in a hundred

Well shall it kindle the light of life?

Had I been you- O ruler of heaven!

Seated on the chariot of wind

Invisibly you have cleaved

Life into innumerable crevices..

The last signs of life blurring

You who bring vast disasters

Bow in your courtyard the seeds

Who like slaves bow to their masters..

O you the chief solemn violinist

Who guards the leaves into their end

In a later time bring jail and mist

O you arranged of a majestic musical!

Those whom you've introduced

With your congregated spirit

Regularly your prayers they mused

In the Carmel of the 'Muse..'

You who incarnate thousand times

Unto this Earth to show your presence

And do hold the authority of carnage

Of infinite withering leaves and thence..

For the good you do reappear

To bring in lost drops of dew

You're responsible to for spring

Yet are revered by very few!

August rush

The wheezing winds bring with it

Tiny icicles of pleasure

The whiplash of thunder and

Uninterrupted moments of leisure

The mellifluous rattle of showers

Revive the dull lethargic Earth-

Into a plethora of greens-

A quintessential rebirth.

A million sun kissed drops descend

Each iridescent as a star

A routine nonchalant epiphany

Uniting zenith in petrichor.

In the concrete architecture

The fauna seeks refuge

The incessant rains for them is

A harbinger of deluge

The cacophonous frogs beget

The ultimate paragon of joy

The rainbow arched beautifully

In the prism of the sky

Clouds masquerade the solar wrath

Promising us liberation

Satiating the thirsty souls

Ending the plight of starvation

For the 'taken' ones August is

A bewitched romantic enchantment

For the sore eyes of forlorn

It is a sermon of dissent....

Enough!

Crossing the threshold in the twilight hour,

Still revives within me unwanted memories sour.

The media headlines screeching in my head -

Over exaggerated though - it makes me afraid.

"How would I be able to distinguish good from evil?

How was i to reckon well wisher from devil?

Those monsters were everywhere with prying eyes,

Voracious hunting dogs in innocent sheep's disguise.

Those haunting wilted spirits, dressed in shades of grey;

Accompanying everywhere. Non-existently foray..

Into my subconscious - reigning the resident fears-

Capturing my thoughts and jilting with jeers-

Satiating their never ending, lustful greed,

Or disfiguring the beauty of life with drops of acid.

What if? This question crumbled my confidence,

Society questioning my character - my very existence."

With all these fears clouded in my head,

Accumulating all the thoughts I move ahead.

Still with no available option I cross the threshold,

Into the pitch dark where ominous things could unfold.

Jinxed to be a girl in a patriarchal society,

Where 'events' grab eyeballs and some fake pity.

I reminded myself I was a girl - incarnation of bloodthirsty Goddess,

An enchantingly dangerous chaos of mess.

With a knife stud in the edge of my sleeve,

The hearts of societal demons I'm ready to cleave.

If any of the cacophonous wolves ever try to glare,

I'm not gonna just stand and stare,

I'm not gonna just stand and stare..

The image

One dark night down the stairs I went,

the same old bunglow we took on rent

I noticed a faint, freckled black image,

the size of a normal mousetrap cage

It followed me like an apparition,

the environment transcended into a haunted mansion

My shaking legs broke into a run,

some confused nuisances voiced in unison

The current went off; I was all alone,

the sole light coming in the form of a cone

Extinguished lanterns creaking past,

the jinxed image approaching fast

A grandfather's clock struck one o' clock,

my voice choked but the vision didn't block

What an odyssey did it seem,

a concoction of horror's frightful realm

The owls intermittently hooted and flew,

ferociously the howling winds blew

Thunderstorm, lightening, fearsome rain-

all my bravery dissolved again

I managed to come off the stairs,

those images now appeared in pairs

The breeze vaunted and bats flew,

the pitch sheer darkness also grew

The church bells knelled and rung,

a faraway musician perhaps sung

Stars eclipsed by loathing clouds,

the crazily taken whining hounds

Wind chimes, banshees squealed,

spine chilling episodes revealed

Werewolves began to evilly grin,

like when snow kissed winters begin

Signs of death appeared all across,

veiled night angels carrying crimson floss

They chanted ominously and touched,

I losing my pulse- crouched

One of them flung affront grabbed my head,

in a freaky, ghostly voice to me said-

"Welcome to our world, hold your breath;

Do you remember the cause of your death?"

Halloween's

An eve of commemoration of the dead ancestors,

To pay tribute to the departed souls,

Celebrating the spirit of

Dedicated to the dead, saints, martyrs,

A day of remembrance of all faithful departed,

A night of vigilance cum 'trick-o-treat'ing,

With Celtic roots, it emerges in the liturgical year,

Decked with spooky themed costume parties,

Making jack-o'-lanterns, lighting bonfires,

Apple bobbing, divination, scary story telling,

A day of abstinence, lighting candles on the graves,

In sweet remembrance to the times of togetherness,

Culminating with offerings of food or crops,

Ending in scrying, mirror gazing, guising,

Spreading fun by imitative sympathetic magic,

Some attractions lying in dream interpretation,

A ray of optimism in decaying dark of winter,

Pumpkins, candy shaped like skulls, pumpkins, bats,

Roasted pumpkin seeds, sweet corn, soul cakes,

Apple pie, Bloody Mary for the extreme foodies,

An overall depiction of merger of joy in grief,

Reminding the co-existence of good and evil,

A traditional emphasis on the essence of life,

Annually celebrated on the last day of October..

Realization

The dense marsh of clouds always ignited within me,

The keenest desire to know what lies entwined beyond them.

I was born to be a free bird, painting the effervescent imagery of my fantasyland.

Little known to the bars of society rising around me, clasping me,

The chains of tradition, the weight of malice confining my wings,

I was a seeker, curious to know of what lies hidden beyond those candyfloss clouds,I didn't realize what was engulfing my dreams.

Until -Caged, I was, bleeding profusely in the scars pricked a thousand times,A million times humiliated at the failures borne out of my efforts,

The overcrowded society pelting stones - annotated with words, jeers, laughs,

I lay there screaming, my screeches disappear in the commotion,No one to lend me a positive communication, to take me out of the chaos,

They burn my vibrant, prancing dreams into a heap of ash,

I wish I was a phoenix to revive my dreams, my identity from the ashes;

Still helpless, resilience drawing me to the end of life,

Was it the end to a tale of woes? Was the ultimate about to come?

I see infinity blackening onto me, the whirlwind of circumstances,

The hovering hurricanes of a blurred, troubled past,

The smog of doubts blurring my hindering confidence,

The mist of ill luck, thoughts of failure grasping me in their firm, frightful grip.

The lost opportunities haunting me like banshees, 'I cannot' echoing in my head,

Still, I rise, still, I rise, for I know I must rise above,

Above all prejudices, above all the clouds of pessimistic assumptions,

I must rise, for beyond the clouds could I see my rainbow of achievements.

I must rise for the ones jeering down wanting me to give up,

Rise above the fears, the falsely misleading philosophy,

I must rise to prove them wrong, my inner demons,

Satanic society, everyone who's against me, envying my slightest celebration,

I must rise for I don't belong here, I must - Rise. Rise. Rise.

The expanse of Sunkissed skies arching the zenith welcome me,

Occasionally turning into a multitude hues of blue,

I, rise above, ignorant of the fate bought to me by my abandoned destiny,

Unable to figure out things dawning upon me, the cosmos engulfed in mystical enchantment,

The tunnel of darkness dissolving into an era of luminescence,

Bringing to me the vastness of the skies I'd longed for so long,

Finally, I gleam with pride, yet not letting it take charge of me,

Faraway, I could see the fast-approaching Lords of Destiny, each with a bejewelled halo

Showering upon me the shimmering fruits of success.

My gaze goes down, no commotion, no jeers, no wrongdoers, not accusations,

Only an ocean of followers - my followers - ready to shower flowers once I descend.

Some thorns of my past smirk in satirical amusement...!

Commuovere

Be not the schwellenangst chained in your prison of life,

Be a eleutheromaniac with the fernweh fire of freedom,

Baffled yet enchanted bt the serendipity of the glaciars,

Or a nemophilist lulled by the mellifluous komorebi of leaves,

Wishing to unravel the mystic secret beauty of the woods.

Be a fascinated vagrant awed by the stories of every unfamiliar passerby

Or lured by the touch of retreating waves in the tranquility of the moon,

Or a seeker wandering towards an undefined destination -

Still numinous over the vales of lush green flora.

Because solivagant who believes in crossing stereotypical thresholds.

A saudade may wet the eyelashes treasuring wanderlust -

But let that not astray you from your expedition,

Be a wayfarer and unhesitatingly explore novelty.

For the ocean calls for the goal-thirsty thalassophile;

Nature donning the bruanous skies, the iridescent rain imagery -

Let your heart throb with resfeber whilst drenched in nostalgia,

Let onimism eclipse your selcouth of self discovery,

Extinguishing the hireath of yugen from your dismal mind.

For, it's when the traveller leaves 'a home', can he find 'the home',

Let the hodophile within take the ambiguous path..

Love

Every fading day,

dissolves into ambiguity.

Like a vagrant flower,

searching it's traces,

in the thorny marshes -

willing to find its pieces,

that'll make it a whole;

in exchange for being

unapologetically pierced

by the ruthless 'tyrants',

giving their floral prey

it's desired destiny...

Isn't it the very same,

when love is to end....?

Escape

Words, not emotions

twinkle in your eyes;

dreams, not we, unite

in those moonless nights.

Because, you were never reality,

just a means to escape;

an escapade you are,

perfectly trained to distract me,

your eyes are magic.

Lock them into mine

Will you?

Lipogram

They say my verses stay stale

Without mentioning your name

As though you, a popular art

My one and only claim to fame

So I thought to exclude from here

The initial letter which forms your name

And affirm I've moved on in life

Away from being your distressed dame

Say, how this poem feels to you

Now that it's bereft of your trace

But yes, I do re-discover now

My long lost charm and grace

Sans you I'm more liberated

From the burden I once used to treasure

Hadn't I met you how I'd have realised

The true aspects that lend me pleasure ?

Mind

A never ending symphony of playful emotions,

A melancholy of stringed remembrances,

A beautiful solitary curious expedition,

A ballad of counterrevolutionary struggles,

An evolving experience of experimentation,

A start point of overthinking thoughts,

A sentimental continent of attachments,

A retelling of traditional altercations,

A sanctified sanctum of beautiful lyrics,

A tale of withering and fading opportunities,

A heapful of grief-stricken incomplete stories,

A burial place for zillion guilty regrets,

My mind isn't just a mind, it's poetry in free-verse

Take me back

My feet take me backwards into the by lane of memories

A place which witnessed my secrets and infamous stories

The days started with assemblies, ending in sleeping classes

The Wednesday classes being a favorite among the masses

Deadlines included the due date of returning library book

Getting promoted to the next class was a matter of fluke

Moral class gave values, science fair gave wings to imagination

English plays gave the orators an opportunity of narration

We made friends and equally foes during basketball matches

And interchanged positions in the subsequent football clashes

Winning the house trophy was everyone's easy claim to fame

Passing chits, pen fights or footsie was a timepass indoor game

Maths bought algebra and unforgivably disastrous marks

Every topper's grade was sure to garner envious remarks

Bullying the weak and fearing the rowdy healthiest guy

Getting called by teacher to solve equations made us cry

Mocking the teachers and mimicking each other we all grew

From nursery to tenth - how strikingly fast the time flew!

Those fleeting, busy corridors permanently etched in minds

Visualizing our own tiny cornered space - a flashback rewinds

Infinite were quarrels, naughtiest follies and truest friends

Students who argued with teachers set the coolest trends

Inspection bought chills, vacations imbibed us with sadness

We didn't even know when it became our second address

The gatherings, the extempore, sports, the endless debates

An ocean of nostalgia treasured behind clinking school gates

Once the road most taken; it's rusticity still steals my breath

I still have a relation, an affinity to it's soothing warmth

It's every brick is evident of friendships, our growing years

Failures which we've experienced in hushed, unsaid, silent tears

Results teared eyelashes, parents meet was a common terror

Pre boards, project assignment submission - a reason of horror

It has seen people who've stayed through every thick and thin

In flourish and fade, in sunlight and shade, in defeat and win

The games period decided every 'sportsman's' favorite weekday

EVS was a craze, craft class taught us the art of modelling clay

My heart overflows and unrevealed tears find their escape

Reminiscing the days of our innocent, idiotic, childish jape

Engraved in my mind is its bittersweet yet soothing essence

Memoirs like souvenirs lay entwined in my sweet remembrance

Shadows of the past

The haunting wilted spirits,

dressed in shades of grey;

Accompanying everywhere.

Non-existent. Still foray..

Into the subconscious

reigning the resident fears-

Capturing our thoughts

and jilting with jeers-

Challenging the demons to

tear the mask which shields,

Negativity in positive moulds.

Yet trust, it yields..

But deceit being evident

in its blood and veins,

Joy being away from

the reservoir of pains,

Shadows not only haunt,

they even know to heal

Your dark deep wounds

if you promise to reveal

You torture yourselves

to hide the cracks, broken pieces

The afflictions, the irreparable sorrow,

and the crevices..

Our shadows command our lives.

Acquaint them.

All the sorrows then

they will unpaint them.

Beknowest of the pros

which revelation shall bring

Without the departing autumn,

how we'll have spring?

Afterthoughts

We loved with a love which was more than love

A boon which angels bestow

A reward that heavens endow

Not the entire world but

Only you and me know

With every passing second

Which tends to grow

Incomplete yet unconditional

Immortally mysterious

Yet divinely sublime......

We loved with a love which was more than love

Free-verse

Let my words flow free.. without being restricted into,

Self defined verses.

Let emotions be boundless, and be limitlessly,

Scattered in ink.

Let my imagination.. not be caged within,

A defined length of paper.

For if I wish to write, the universe shall fall short.

And nd the slightest particle of dust, shall have the touch of my words.

Every rumbling river, shall flow to my melancholy.

The falling autumn leaves, shall recite my musings.

The undying specks of stars, shall have my spark.

The raging wildfire, will roar with my poems.

Let the enchantress of time, metamorphose my verses,

Into free-verse

You search me in places

You search me in places

But still you don't find

The one who's residing

In your very own mind

And here I lie

Imprisoned in stone

Witnessing the doom

Of the creation of my own

Atheist or not

It's your view

Then in my name

Why do you argue

Please set me free

I'm omnipresent

And abide by your

Human temperament

Don't let faith

Blind your vision

Release your soul from

The chains of superstition

Days spent not talking

Descending down the zenith, the sun seems to rest.

After a busy schedule, inviting patience for a test..

Hours pass like years

And days like decades

But none of us show

A single sign of regret

Was it really love?

Thoughts erupt in my mind, like a forest on fire.

Into the trench of sorrow, distraught I retire..

I left without explaining

For you to make your

'Self invented interpretations' -

You seemed to care

The very least..

The days of togetherness, went past like flutterflies.

The times of fornlorn, infinitely cast in the skies..

With all activity stats

Put under the wraps

Of a never dying ego

Our non existent relation

Breathes it's last.

The twinkling stars have, their muse in the moon.

And I stand here all alone, for dawn to arrive soon..

I'm left alone in dark

With my ocean of regrets

You with your ambitions

Don't care to dwell

Over 'mere' proceedings.

Nights no longer exist, in true companionship.

They remain as reminders, of a died relationship..

Just a tiny green spot

Could illuminate a ray

Of positive hope

But you don't dare to give

'US' a last chance.

Neither me nor you or we, no one was really at fault.

It's the depth of separation, which mounts to its exalt..

Florets

Entangled within the thread of evening

The little flowers try to bloom

White as milk, their touch as silk

They are so born to doom

Their presence like diamond

Burning in the setting sun

Delicate as glass, sweet as floss

Swaying in unperturbed unison

Growing in the vine destiny

Determined to reach the sky

Tiny as dots, tied in knots

Spreading joy before they die

Petalled in an uneven hexagon

Architectured in a geometry

With petals long, thorns which throng

Withering in a just hours three

Their fragrance eternal and divine

The natural perfume of Lord

Drenched in mist, caged in cyst

Instrumental players on their accord

Reigning freely, they fall at dawn

The fall intended to lend newty

Their life is less, we must confess

They're a palanquin of beauty

A bouquet of dewy tenderness

Emerging in the month of rain

Enchantresses shy, they then dry

For future generations to sustain

Learn from the oceanic thoughts

Which they leave behind

Ending mighty grief in a jiff

Fulfilment in a life we'd find

The sudoku of life

What's life other than the toughest sudoku puzzle?

Scarcely filled at the will of the supernatural 'puzzle setter'

Raw, unsettled, partial, mystical, unsolved, tiring

A logical, combinatorial decision placement game..

Where a single repetitive verse accuses you of copy

Every overlapping stanza is a potential plagiarist case

You couldn't hum a catchphrase with carefree ease

Nor deliberately fit yourself in society preset stereotypes..

The ultimate objective lies in completing blank squares

With stories of supposed Success, Optimism Compassion

Adorned with Faith, Benevolence, Relations and Altruism

With some minimal touch ups of Leadership and Beauty'..

But for those who fail to fill them the only solution being

To end the ongoing game and again starting afresh

Because you can't strikethrough filled numbers in life

Leaving the game incomplete is the only escape..

Suicide in other terms they say is self motivated death

But initiated with multiple must 'fit in' standards of society

The rules of sudoku when applied in the game of life

It is bound to see premature closure and termination

Calendar of dreams

The autumn of failure ready to cast a curse

And shatter our decisions or even worse

Sow the seeds of self doubt and unending fear

Automatically ripping the conscience to think clear

Already injured by failure- an utter bitter reality

A wretched fate bewitched by negativity..

Julian accord mandates it to start with January

Recovering albeit wounded by the past's fury

It would be no exception for even me to start

From this very point, devicing resolutions- a fine art

The calendar of my dreams would enclose within

All the previous experiences- much to my chagrin..

The Valentine's month would beautifully engrave

An epitaph of withered disappointment on its grave

Some wistful thoughts, some mindful conversations-

Star-crossed Lavenders

Its rosette skeletons, self wounded expectations

Few tattered icicles of snowflakes, sugarcoated love

 Which menacing Devils of Karma unfailingly bestow..

March would accompany with it endless baffling duties

The choice between heartache or faded opportunities

Ashes of ancient wilted, charred, unresolved enigma

Bravely seeking to challenge negative societal stigma

Which believes that not all here are meant to achieve

The dreams which we all tend to toss time and again-

However hard we try to shut them- it's afterall all in vain..

Spring again casts the spell of majestic enchantment

Clearing the mess of fallen leaves from 'Autumn's' vent

Coloring our thoughts with flutterflies of hope and regret

Which we encase with utmost reverence in heart's closet

The means of achieving those dreamy goals is left to us

Engaging us in planning the execution of our magnum opus..

Summers bring with them not only piercing scars of sunshine

Busy mornings, chaotic mess which none can genuinely incline

It is frustrating to keep trying on and miserably fail everytime

In life, not all joyfully mesmerizing stanzas can equally rhyme

Challenges are not enemies- just opportunities in disguise

Which enhance our latent potential- a fact known to the wise..

The hardwork of summers is nullified by rains of fulfillment

As germinating sowed seeds of pain eternally reap achievement

Little infant steps of success turn into stepping milestones

And the strivers feel pride in hearing occasional envious groans

The empress of time smirks wickedly at the face of fate

We are headstrong on achieving more than what we get

 Continual rains have been customarily linked to ruin

The crystal castle of glass which got erected too soon

Floods of disastrous ego clashing its delicate walls

Owing to the fleeting masterpiece that success is - it befalls

Right from ground zero again we ought to restart

Success isn't a naive bride to last till death do apart..

Having learnt a tough lesson that-success doesn't matter

Given its fragile temporary nature- don't allow it to flatter

Success gains significance if we learn to live with it-

We begin with with unadulterated reaffirming grit

This time resolved to not let it escape very easily

We sketch the blueprint of dreams- a bit cautiously..

Following dreams has never been a cakewalk for anyone

Be it an ignorant novice or a well versed experience one

The way that leads to it is full of hovering possibilities

An ever increasing dark cavern of plausible difficulties

Hence it becomes very challenging to carve a niche

When every intersection invites you to leave and ditch..

The unfaltering urge to reinvent yourself is all it takes

No journey can be forced speedily, it requires breaks

Optimism, positive self talk, 'never give up' attitude

Are the known secrets to reach a certain altitude

It takes a very dedicated, stubborn knight to go afar

And stay unfazed and permanent as a pole star..

But if one is truely ardently devoted to aim high

And follow the roadmap routinely, we can reach 'the sky'

Nothing is impossible, the word itself says 'I'm possible'

Life in itself is a mystery where everyone is capable

Just focus on it intensely and let nothing let you sway

Every charming, alluring angel- you must force faraway..

When we reach there after turmoil of painstaking pasts

We'll try to preserve 'the hard earned' as long as it lasts

Achievements and the varying protocols of achieving them

Dont follow a specified path; for all they aren't the same

Know your strengths and touch up your weaknesses first

This way you'll save your fantasy bubble a premature burst..

The calendar of dreams, of aims, of targets, of goals

Has to be proofread and bereft of foolish loopholes

It's a conifer bearing fruits of constant perseverance

And deserved by all of us - at alternating instance

The days, hours, minutes, seconds and moments

Have to be invested carefully- or else one laments.

A lover's curse

A love, did lose beacause of thee

Who is't nev'r did understand its beauty

For thee which wast a temporary game

Wast mine only cause of existence

What wilt thee knoweth of love?

Doth stars knoweth of dew gouts,

Thee a naughty blinded wretch !

And I a neverending flote of lustre..

Haiku

Intermittent clouds

Drenched desires

A haiku pops

The thundering whiplash

Dripping ecstatic icicles

A petrichor of union

The dent in his cheeks

The blush in her eyes

Reveal many secrets

The exhausting greens

The first sunrays

Plot a tale of love

Endnote

You left me enshrined in loneliness

Devastating my effervescence in a tiff

Unsuccessfully though, I fake happiness

While my heart is drenched in grief

From the spark of resentment is

Born the fire of revolution.

From the jeers of "you can't" should be born

The resolution of "I will".

Mirrors

"If mirrors could talk,

They would narrate -

How much every day,

We underestimate,

Our latent potential;

And stay aligned,

To shallow compliments:

Leaving behind our inner beauty,

Which we forage in search of,

A mere mirage...!"

Notes

..Their name, habits, passion, words, everything is engraved on your heart, which cannot wiped out by feigning ignorance.. Unsaid and unacknowledged love injures the most. Love is the swansong of life. A dream, an enchantment, a blessing, a boon, a miracle, a beautiful bereavement, love is the supremacy of destiny in our life and acceptance is the stamp..

..Like poetry, love too, cannot be left incomplete with the mark of 'unrequited' on it, love seeks forever..

I'm blissful on this occasion to have been gratified by serving you O readers! I'm humbled by your recitals and blessed by your servitude.. Now I owe none !!